THE DOWNPOUR

The rain falling so heavy outside

I'm all covered and dressed but can still feel the cold inside

The sound of the pour so loud and hard

Lucky for him with his woman or mistress

For the scorn of the cold causes him no distress

And the downpour wins him much needed caress

DARK DAYS HEAVY HEARTS AND PAINFUL NIGHTS

Dark days, cold nights and heavy hearts

To summarize these few years past

Young, innocent minds needing love and care

Left to vile monsters to do as they deem fair

Curses, rebukes and scolds forced to bare

Penance for sins never declared

Harsh painful lashes upon faultless conscience

Voices too brutal for sacred innocence

Constant labors to cast down and humiliate

What vile thing for a child to feel neglect

AN EPISTLE TO MY MOTHER

I want to write an epistle

To my sweet beloved mother

To narrate a poetic account

Of the happenings during her absence

Of the goings since her departure

Of our existence without hers

But my brain withholds memories from me

To relive those crucial times it won't let me

I'm stuck with a pen in my fingers all powerless

Staring into blank paper, my thinking all pointless

Every passing hour of everyday I hold a funeral

For the millions of poems that perish in this head

That never gets to meet paper through any ink form

The poems I compose every second as I walk

Those I compose in class, in movies, in meals

But circumstantially never see the light of day

Who to blame for these grave happenings

Mine super- fast brain or these sadly human hands

One too fast for the other, the other too slow for one

God I need hands as quick as mine brain

Or is it my brain needing to pace with my fingers

Either at least this one never cut throat And is here written though composed far on the road

Yes proud really I am, for I am one grave less in this head.

Nothing makes my head roll in musical gay
Than the sound of nice African beats and sounds
That make you want to move your body in dance
And forget everything and walk the express lane to heaven

And we do it all in all languages, given us by our fathers
Xhosa, Rwandese, Ghanaian, Swahili, Congolese
And by musicians undoubtedly the best the earth will ever produce
Franco, Brenda Fascie, Makeba, Les Wanyika, Alicios, Kidum
Mapenzi, Mamou, Amigo, Ndihambanawe, Lengoma, Usiende

They call us the Dark Continent
Have they heard our music?
Have they seen us dance?
Have they seen us play our instruments?
Have they seen how good we are at theirs?
Not only is Africa the cradle of mankind
Its definitely the birthplace of music.

A life without purpose, is one like a circus

It could leave you in tatters, if you don't make planners

Six jobs like a juggler, not one drop that's a failure

But what's life without a purpose, no sense still like a circus

Call here call there, deadline to beat and children to care

This that email to share, to fail to finish this job don't dare

Many times feels unfair, that it's too much to do u can't bare

But what's life without cares, it's only best that we all prepare

Working so hard to make money, forget bout your family forget bout your honey

And is it all not funny, you look into the mirror and "Goddamn is that a

belly" So you work to get skinny, and curse the world for making you a fatty

But whats life without a purpose, take it on by its horns and bring it down like a hummer

WHEN I SEE YOU

The softness of a slow piano tune

The softness of the full moon bright

The softness of the eyes in an infant's look

And the same of the waters of a slow flowing

rook Is the softness in my heart when I see you.

Terrible happening it was,

What I saw this night in my sleep

I've seen many bad things

But this! Mine eyes had never set sight

A sin too vile any soul to bare

Sharp screams renting the evening air

From a lass, victim of the painful sin

Everything about that evening seemed sinister

Not even the setting sun was of consolation

He seemed to paint the sky an evil crimson

Calm as though unable to act the wind was

Like it also stood a distance and watched things unfold

Eight men standing around the poor soul, towering

Some of whose acquaintance I knew too well

Each waiting for their turn to unleash spears

And shove them into her young womanhood.

Witnessing one corrupt the helpless girl

I could read regret on the faces of his accomplices

But they all had a set out purpose

A goal that must be achieved, must

Regret would have its time later

It's not my wish to be detailed in this

For the obvious, too much filth involved

One was done and quietly walked off

Widely accomplished but full of regret

Poor girl was to relive the suffering

Seven times over that fateful evening.

I see these small kids stare at me

Blank looks sharp eyes total naivety

Complete mystery what their thoughts may be

What kind of stranger this young man be

They remind me of a time not too long ago

When my passion for success burnt hotter than a volcano

When id admire every wealthy chap I saw on the go

And prayed hard that my destination would that direction go

How I stared at their expensive cars and flashy lives

How everything they owned and had, I wanted to have

How I wanted the mansions, private jets and vehicles they drove How

I dreamt of gliding through the sky of wealth as a dove

Every day I saw myself driving a range rover vogue

Every day I saw myself in a mansion on the ocean shore

Every day I saw the expensive furniture, wear and shores

And every day these images woke me up with a will to live another day

Like these naïve kids I used to stare once

I just don't know what they think when they glance

Maybe like me they admire and see in life a chance

And probably one day these images will wake them up with a will to live another day.

And if these images ever become their dreams

I'll probably never come to know these things

Because like those who are now part of my biggest dreams

I'll be too busy chasing my most daunting dreams

Pretty girl lost in the woods

Everyone loved you here or is it?

Your mum weeps day and night

For her little girl who now must be in fright

Her eyes too sore for any more tears

Her heart too feeble for any more fears

It's clear you didn't run oh dear

So who took this girl away from here

It's too cold for a little lass out there

Not even an hour would a grown man dare

What's to say of a teen with no care

Is it your body we're looking for Alison?

Or are you curled up somewhere shaking cold?

Waiting for us to put thee in thy mother's fold?

If you are then hold on and be very bold.

For we are coming to you fast with a shoal

To protect you from the harsh blistering cold

A country of chaos yes we are

We think we are moving but no we're not

We think we are genius but we know it's false

We're ruled by a bunch of tricksters and immorals

Who lie to us everyday like we're all fools Kenya we are a falling

tower, who doesn't know that If someone doesn't condemn, we're all condemned.

Have I told you how mad you drive me?

Have I told you that I close my eyes?

Every time I speak on the phone with you

That your beautiful smile leaves me speechless

That thoughts of you have rendered nights sleepless

That I crave your kiss so bad

That your absence makes me sad

That I can't wait till you are back

Coz I want to wrap the tightest hug around you.

If my sadness reaches not your remorse

If my frailty doesn't inject you with cause

If my sickly form opens not your eyes to your flaws

Then let me tell you I'm a pretty little suffering crow

I never chose my blackness at all

But in all the earth it's all I've got

And I pray that in your heart you plot

To remove my suffering the whole lot

I don't care if you shoot me in the throat

Or if you drown me down a moat

I just want to be free of this rot

So please take my suffering take the whole lot

Castles are hard to build

That's why they're left to kings

But I'm gonna lay stone upon stone

I'm gonna work as one on the throne

Till I see it all built and grown

Everything surrounded by a big ol' moat

Where hundreds of crocodiles can swim and float

Then furnish the living with expensive seats

And a good huge fireplace where I can stretch my feet

Beautiful carpet to line the floor beneath

Magnificent coffee table where I can take my tea

One balcony facing the world to the west

And another all the way to the east

So every evening I can watch as the sun sets

And in the morning watch it come up in the east

A lion on either side of the entrance door

So that everyday we'll be reminded that weakness is wrong

Whatever made us created us to be social

But sometimes the hearts seeks solitude, away from the

social When it can be quiet and with itself be cordial

When it can relax and rest without sorrow.

I LOVE YOU BILA SIRI

Nakupenda, bila siri

Sina wala simtaki wa pili

Nishakuambia wewe ni mrembo?

Nishakuambia unavyonipa midundo?

A rose I want to wake up to everyday

I never want you to go please stay

Because in your eyes I see my future in play

Sitaki kuwahi kaa mbali na mwili wako

Joto lote na yote mapenzi yako

Jambo lipi tamu duniani kukuliko

Njoo nikupe busu

Come let me kiss you Pamojatuweusiku

And ill never leave you Unanipatabasamu

Caught by love's curfew

Nakupenda mpenziwangu

You're my babie n I love you

Many times when we walk alone

Especially in the dark night

We hear footsteps aside from our own

As if someone is walking behind us

Someone we never see even when we look

Some say it's Jesus, always with us to protect us

Others say it's those we loved who died walking with us

Others still the devil roaming the night for lonely souls

Many times when about to do wrong

Especially in the dark night

We hear voices aside from our own

As if someone is talking behind us

Someone we never see even when we look

Some say its Jesus always with us to talk to us

Still others the devil roaming the world for weak souls

Many times when the lights are gone

Especially in the dark night

We see forms aside from our own

As if someone is standing behind us

Someone we never see even when we look

Some say its Jesus always with us to stand by us

Others say it's those we loved who died, standing with us

Still others the devil roaming the earth for scared souls

I guess as humans we have to get used

To ghostly beings living among ourselves

Yester night

As I was lost in my own thoughts

I thought of the death of my father

I thought of how it will be

I thought of when it will be

And what it will be that'll cause it

I thought of myself at the funeral

I thought of myself at the funeral

Their shocked faces

Their thoughtful looks

I thought about who will be there

I though about my eulogy of him

I saw myself reading a poem

A poem to eulogize the one who sired me

In one instance I saw myself so weak

Unable to articulate for too many painful sobs

In another I saw myself so strong in spirit

Like his death shook me not the slightest inch.

Best time

To sit alone on a cliff

And hang my legs off the cliff

So close to death yet so alive

To watch the deep valley sink beneath

And the towering hills on either side

To admire the grandeur and marvel the monstrosity To see God in all this

greatness

Coz that's the only way big enough to see it

The endless sky, the deepest valley and the highest hills

Bring in a feeling so great and so hard to explain

A time when I can be alone and depart from the world

A time when I can laugh alone and say to myself every word

A time when I don't have to impress neither live by anyone rules

A time when I can close my eyes and see myself glide in the sky so blue

Open my heart gladly without fear of criticism

Talk to myself loudly without accusations of egotism

In company with trees and the wind who don't judge my agnosticism

Yes this is the best time, to myself, dealing not even with pluralism

Church

Where we worship with witches

Where we commune with demons

Where we associate with vampires

And we know not of their presence among us

This place where we sit with beasts and talk of angels Where

we listen with snakes about tales of heaven

Where we dream of eternity, sitting right next to death

This place a home of vanity where in unison we all finish, AMEN!

Adopted from The Originals sn.1 ep.13 Beginning service.

ITS ONLY WHEN YOU WAKE UP EARLY ENOUGH

Its only when you wake up early enough

That you realize the sterningness of the rising sun

Its only when you look close enough

That you see the lines too faint for normal eyes

Its only when you want something bad enough

That the universe conspires to grant you the desire

So like will.i.am lyricizes it in a song.

"don't wait for luck, dedicate yourself and you gon' find yourself.

I feel this place has met its purpose
It fed this insatiable urge that I had
To be on my own and think to myself
To talk to myself and meditate
To think of my existence and my priorities
To recall my past, arrange my present and my future too
To audit my heart and mind and look deep in.

I poured out my heart the much I needed
Revisited some scars now like stars in the sky
A month of peeping deep and writing
Sometimes with my mind even fighting
Disturbing long sleeping demons
Letting open Pandora's Box in my head
Letting all those ill and painful thoughts fly around

Anyway this place gave me what I needed
Now I'm done with all the solitude
Now I need to go back to that altitude
Those highs.

MAYBE

I know what I'm supposed to do
I know I'm supposed to get up
Do what I'm supposed to do
But
Maybe I can lay back a bit
Maybe I can spread my legs a bit
Maybe for a minute I can shut these eyes
And let my mind wonder wildly
And think about that girl
About her small sweet lips
Maybe I can think, no imagine
Myself
Rich as a king
Travelling the earth, walking on mars
No that became boring.
This Neyo tune sounds relaxing
Maybe I should think about that girl again
Maybe she likes me, maybe she doesn't
Me, I've known never to cast the net too far
At least not for one fish
Today I saw another fish
And thought maybe I should cast my net
Just throw caution to the wind And lift that net to the sea.

THERE WAS SO MUCH NOISE

There was so much noise
Plus it's not like I had a choice
There was so much I felt I needed to voice

So much I needed to do yet I wasn't poised
I recall how I decided to begin this hustle
The things I opted to do to free me from this tussles
How I plotted to achieve glory and one day rattle.

But just but
I forgot to do one thing more important than all else
I forgot to do the one thing I know to do best
I forgot to write
To pen down the pinnacles I plan to reach
To ink the objects of my desire
To realize the exact note and pitch.

Now I return dreams all new, good ol' crew
Ideas not few, ready for the money ready to accrue.

THE PEN IS POWERFUL

The things we do with pens
We destroy nations
We bring down kings
We inspire endless wars
We approve iniquity
We disintegrate houses
We condemn prosperity
We catapult calamity
And detest prosperity
We fill brains with ideas
That open Pandora's boxes everywhere
We inflict doubt and fear

And cause faint hearts to tear.
Unparalleled is the pen's might
It would be justice to call it a god.

I WILL KEEP WRITING

This writing hangs on balance
A settled heart a settled mind
But I am anchored on a side
And all free on the other
Twisted, bent, angled
And in no position to do that, write
But I'm a prolific writer
I will write about this imbalance
I will write about my burdened heart
I will write about my troubled heart
I will keep writing and writing
Even about my very own imbalance.

I HAVE COME TO LEARN

I have come to learn
That no single head on earth
Is better than that and another together
One man is better than none
Two men are better than one
Even the good book is one
Telling of the story of men in Babel
Who together would be in heaven
Had that deity not struck.

This bottle before me
This bottle of liquor
I sit here staring at this bottle
As a chemist stares at red turning blue
I'm reflecting on it, I'm thinking about
Tall and huge 750 milliliters
Red cap, clear glass, label at the centre
It's crystal clear, because of emptiness or fill, I know not
This bottle of liquor
I have many problems this day
I can drown them all right?
I can forget all of 'em this moment can't i?
Yes I can and maybe I will
I can't see the label, can't see the logo
But I know what its slogan says
"Drink till death" Death!
I love death, I've always loved death
Why not drink, why not?
I would know what the drank man feels
When staggering and falling into mud puddles
At least he's closer to life's best part, death.

I LOVE MY LITTLE GIRL BEFORE SHE'S BORN

I love my little girl before she's even born
I love her and Eros can testify I do
I see her pretty face and cheeky smile
I see her falling asleep in these daddy arms
The way she crawls all over the house
And tries to say to me things I can't make out
The way she closes her tiny eyes in my arms
And breaths slow with a nose like her mum's
The sight of my little baby in her sleep
One I want to hold for eternity indeed
I tell her "chum" baby "chum"
And I get a sweet kiss from her little lips
I've seen her, felt her, I've known her
So when you come baby, know
I loved you before you were even born

I was so drowned in these waters of deeds
I forgot to see the world like I used to
I was so run over by this convoy of troubles
I forgot to look back and keep those memories true
I was so blown off by this whirlwind of activity
My love for the good times almost slipped out of these fingers.

THAT'S LIFE

If the shadow is becoming darker
Then the sun must be getting brighter
If the night seems to be getting longer
Then the morning is definitely closer
Death will come whether you worry or not
Fate will happen whether you hurry or not
So fill your days with life and be sorry not
Spend it all on joy and don't spare even a note
Watch the sun come up every start of a day
And when he retires to sleep down beyond the hills
Follow the Niagara and fourteen as far as they flow
Walk the Great Wall of China experience man's might
Swim the Dead Sea and defy a law of nature
This is why we should live
Not for food and shelter
But for the moon and pleasure
Not with pain and pressure
But for might and treasure.

I, LIKE THE WIND

To be like the wind

That's all I want and will
Flow where I wish glide where I feel
Whistle when I want, or be quiet and all still
Flow into every crevice I find, sometimes have no mind Have the
sea bow at my feet
Make the trees dance at my whim
To always be felt but rarely be seen,
Not be controlled, never be provoked
Always a god always on top.
Many times calm and relaxing
Giving people pleasure in the basking
Meeker than a lamb
Other times a ruthless master
Killing everything on the way, everything

THROWN OUT OF HEAVEN, THROWN OUT OF HELL

Drowned
Flown to heaven
Thrown back to earth
Rejected on earth
Sought refuge in hell
Laughed at by the devil
And because he likes a good laugh,
Rejects me too.
Just to see where I'd end up
Refused in heaven, in hell
Not accepted on earth, not wanted
Even sinners feel some warmth
The warmth of God's hate
The warmth of the devil's mock
Someone feels something about them
For the coldness in this place
Can't be explained by heaven
Can't be fought even by hell's fire
This cold is not eternal
This cold is severe
These are all understatements.

WHY I WRITE

Is that not what makes us human?
That in our chest called feeling?
Which entangles hearts at the sight of suffering
Which wets our eyes at the sight of others' tears
Which freezes our being at the mention of death
This, forces my pen to the job
To tell paper what my heart says
To ease a delicate heart of heaviness
To rid paper of blankness and give it
Longed and much needed purpose
Its because I write
That my heart is light
This is why I write
To give purpose to life
To give purpose to ink and white
To boast intellectual might
To condemn what's not right.

Things in the past i put them at bay,

My redeemer he liveth he'll redeem me if He may,
Bury the hatchet i believe them for they say,

For while the sun is up, it's noble to make hay,
Clinging to this might leave me in dismay,
My future so bright no want to live life astray,

Forgive them, who caused me pain that led me to pay,

I believe they can for they can't make it a foray,
And make a pursuit, then convict me to bay,
Maybe once for a long time my conscience I not betray

IN YOUR EYES

Appearing as round as they are,
Tenderly and passionately I sign when you stare,
Treating them like mine my candid pleasure,
For non I've seen having such a glare,
Meek I am so the world must know I care,
Even the flies will commend with a buzz,
Buzz with mesmerizement not just a mare,
Hold me tight my dearest,
Like as if you'll never again,
Let the tears in your eyes freely flow,
For I see a sign in a state of readiness,
Blurring partially your vision,
How I would like to wipe them out,
Lest my chest you want wet.

It's been a while, a while so long,
Longer than the longest sea,
The struggles and the perseverance,
Has fetched me a handsome reward,

Which lives my face in smiles,
My redeemer is so kind,
The kind of a great manifestation,
Now it's time to give my laments a ride,
To the land over the mountains,
Far away that they'll never return.

From the confines of this room, where I sit,
In the offprint, my head deeply buried,
Supporting my chin, with such unstable hands,
Just like the pillars of the gedi remains,
Whiling away some pleasant hours,
Struggling to impart some token of know-how,
With the opportunity of which am bestowed,
But ever mindful of the perils of failure,
I know though, success is in the offing,
For almighty will bless my attempts with good success,
And enjoy the fruits of the aftermath.

REBORN

From the ink of my pen I write,
How I met time to face the waters,
As a sign of purity and initiation,
Trudging along the Stony path downstream,
As the parson open-handedly awaited,
To make a lifetime spiritual advance,
Other voices soared on high in praises,
As long as this put me at bay,

From the evil one's buffeting temptations,

For I imagine freedom's mellow light,
Even the parson witnessed with heartfelt mead,
Any form of phobia for cold vanish in cloud of fear,
But pinning my trust in him drawn me not,

Now the new me, fresh and reborn.

UNDERNEATH

Some perilous situations, deserve to be told,

For they can't forever remain untold,
The many misdeeds that only us it please,
If bare-laid can make us catch a cold,
If the realities are to practically unfold,

Swifter than the moon's sphere,
Such advances subjected only to the bold,
For raw realities of life not to recede,
Before death veils its vital gleam,
And the abyss opens up for us to seek,
The imagination so horrid, so priceless to behold.

THE MONK

All the time I take in the monastery,
Holy books I read that existed before my time,
With researches scientifically that I've made,
The intelligence in my mind engraved,
Hypocrisy has refused to part me ways,
Crossing the red river I want for once,
My generation I long for ardently,
Resurrecting the legendary of my dear men,
Because they legacy they left,
Haunt me day and night,
Same glass they used I want to drink from,
To taste the same liquor they tasted,
Parting with them ways a taboo,
But forgiveness grant me oh! Lord,
For I will be a holy sinner,

With sagging trousers I stagger the lonely path,

The bushy hair erect from the roots,
Trousers soaked with liquid of ammonia smell,

Choosing it doesn't whether learned it mind not,
Like a slave in clanking chains am trapped in liquor,
But with full-fledged war I have to fight,
My weakness so strong, I fight to lose,
Now from hand to mouth I feed,
Noisy metallic monsters madly pass me by,
When I limp ignorantly across the road,

They'll run me over some tragic day,
I have not to blame any being,

But curse my limbs that drag me to the den,

For the outcast of the clan I have become.

Bowing in holy manner, a lot with pretense,
Bibles held at acute angle,
The lost to trust, in God they convince,
But at night they are pig in mad,
They're like goat in lion's skin,
They forget as quickly as they can recall,
They preach repentance and patience,
But at night they're pig in the mud,
Like wilting leaves they are not,
They don't perish easily in this life,
For the coward monkey lives long,
Like baby baboon they cling to hypocrisy,
The great gate's slippery you stumble and fall.

BY THE THROB OF THE RIVER

I love the sound of the throbbing river,
The soothing flawless sound of the roar,
Just like the rhythm of an orchestra,
And the endless rattle of the insects,
Constantly chanting melodies to them known,
For the mighty streams ceaseless determination,
The undying might not even by the lurk of aridity,
I feel its pleasure, my distress to carry away,
To set sail my worries to a yonder shore,
The fear of loneliness and earthly tough luck,
A creepy illusion, like an eerie midnight owl.

A PIECE FOR ONE OF MY OWN

Before i start to feel passing of the years,
Before i get someone to dry up my tears,
And get an aid to help me forebear my fears,
Then withhold all the mischievous affairs,
For my conscience this is what it tares
But at all cost, inwardly i have to prepare,
So not to derail in my mind train of ideas,
For all the blows i faced in the yesteryears,
The ceaseless pain, for me so hard to bear,
Caused by my own misgivings but nobody cares,
The world's cruelty proving somewhat unfair,
But at least for one of my own a piece i spare,
When this will come handy for them inspire,

It dates from time immemorial,
Where political rain started hitting us hard,
Harder than smith's hummer on steel,
With the strife embers still soaring on high,
Higher than a nitrogen balloon can go,
Five decades gone by, as we can chiefly remember,
Now anew to open the old gone lesions,
By the two given and gifted, scion of the fallen mighty,
Who still hum tunes of a song danced by their forbearers,
And permit contention in their heart take refuge,
Thus subject the humble shed series of long tears,
Whose strained efforts comfort them the affluent,
With no a whisker of compassion ever thought of,
Now the much stung in depth by the political cold,
Whose sneeze would make the others catch a cold,
Seeks with zeal heed of the burning spear,
So much with attempts without any apparent deterrent,

OUT IN THE COLD

To scribble a piece for someone I love,
Counting the stars so hard to keep count,
To express my love in both pen and paper,

My dear lessee please don't let me down,
For I took my time and might to let you know,

How deep and much my love is for you,
The crickets chipping endlessly besides me,
Might tell for they witnessed maybe when am gone,
Give me the best in your time for am trying my best,

And make my betrothed happy for she does the same,

Gamble and play but don't lose a teeth,

For that pain for me won't be so easy to bear,
Like hitting my head against a hard rock,
It'll tear me apart and perhaps kill me quick.

One day you will grow dark and tall; precise,
Not to dark and not too light though,
Taller than the Napier in the *Savannah*,
The same eyes, shinning in the blink of light,
Time will fly, like a savaged bald eagle,

They'll watch your eyes agape when you speak,

And make series of slow agreeable nods,
When you surpass all odds in your time,

I'll send a guardian angel to watch over you,
Because no love is love than my love,
Time when am done and gone to my maker,
Just when you grow I know you will grow,

EMMY

On that cloud with green walls,
where i met you, my little stranger,
for good reasons, divine and sundry our paths crossed,
I realized i needed you, for some reason i know not,
Coming to know you is like a first kiss so hard to breathe,
With a feeling of shelter and infinite rest,
Your friendliness come whole not halves or thirds,
Our undetermined silence is a flavor to our bond somewhat,
Now we are more than just common friends,
This friendship means more than you'll ever know.

Passion drove when I became one,
Belief was hard to some not even myself,
Poetry for poets now I know am one,
Bubbling not enough but I know I have won,

I won't tire to write not even on hire,
Sky will fall and find me twitching my pen,
Smiling to the stars the drop a surging line,
Lessee will hold it high more than higher maybe,

Time I'll scratch my brain enough and tremble writing longer,
She'll pen it slow, doing a song or something smarter,
Very energetic with ambition doing it all sober,
Love for the pen and paper, kills idle dead as dodo.

MY GOOD GONE FRIEND

You remember your good gone times?
Mine is not too long ago, a year or two,
Now I mourn tears all over this place,
My dearest trusted good gone friend,
You want me mourn all this while,
Why do you let me chock my throat in pain?
Come back to me this one more time,
Endurance is not my cup of tea,
Tell me or of you can't send someone,
Help me take this not for betrayal,
Give me the reason why you break my bones,
Help me pick up myself up I can't take this low,
If you can't show me the way through,
Please don't let me conceive you betrayal,
For trust me this is not the right time,
Bet me! Bet me! Bet me! Brother...

Love from a humbled heart,
Good intentions, deeds that meet needs,
She came with a brilliant smile my betrothed,
We made toasts in the air in merrymaking,
Then you creeped in and brought us perpetual joy,
Your eyes like hers resemble, a life she gave,
My bright beautiful rose a flower,

Ceaseless love from a father surmounts you,

Like appeased heart if an orphaned child

JUST FOR *JENNIE* MY MOTHER

I've longed for this time so long,
To sit down for a while just for *Jennie*,
In the company of my pen and paper,
To scribble something special for she deserve,
Not even a strong waved storm will stop me by,
Never will I even spare time for a cup of tea,
All your time you saw needful when you gave me,
To make me elite to school when you sent me,
The right and wrong you saw helpful when you taught me,
Kindness is of a class i believed when you told me,
Now a piece you see is time I give you,
For no love a love surpasses mama love.

That was the last time though not forever,
That i touched those hands i remember,
Am grateful though to father that i endeavor,
That i try hard with might not to surrender,

That was the last time that she came,
She spoke, i mumbled i almost got lame,
I stared i was scared that i failed to tame,
Those eyes of her's to me full of fame,

That was the last time i tried a whisper,
T'was the last time my eyes had a glitter,
Nowadays they are just as cold as winter,
An emptiness running deep as still water,

This is the last time this long i wallow,
With a heart so heavy and hollow,
This is the last time I cling to the pillow,
Your scent so fresh it chokes to swallow,
This is the last time I choose to be mellow.

During my gray days,
Your good eyes will still flash in my sight as if your 20s,
In your 20s when I met you,
Swore to you, that lessee will have your eyes,
Behind my blurry eyes I see your youthly smile,
Beyond your shivering wrinkles,
I can still feel the static racing to my marrows,
Raising my angled chin to the cloud entangled sky,
Holding some support still,
Swinging my arm flap, stubble legs, my gray days
Oh loathsome days …

CASANOVA

You stared with eyes round and eager,
I tried to evade, your wide smile caught my attention,
Strolling beside me, butterflies bombarding my stomach,
Beauty that can engulf me like a curse,
A flowery band binding me to the earth,
Pursuing the beckoning charm I defy in vain,
Your sweet voice is like summer wind,
creeping from petal to petal.

...with the slim light shadows of the moonlight,
a saw lips of my betrothed, wanting me to water them,
a feeling so rare, just us, the two of us, he held me,
by the neck and planted that charged kiss,
that made me feel like nothing could harm me,
the feeling was so new, and the smell so fresh,
doing it in ways and means i can't deny not to understand,

YOUR MAGIC HANDS

I trust the work of God which came handy,
But oops! I almost stumbled and fell,
How did you do it anyway?
Because I found hope along the way,
I believe you won't leave sometime in May,
Comfort me for you are here to stay,
Acceptance for me was a hard bargain,
For the pleasure and the urges so hard to refrain,
Take my feebly hands alone I can't sustain,
And direct, me to a point I can maintain,
Sooth me with your magic hands and let me feel,
For my sore wounds this is what will heal,
And dance the magic tune with my safe heels.

Many days that you went so callous and cold,
Chilling and petrifying to the bone,
I knew you belonged to me and me to you,
It was hard to try for a second not to think of you,
But the tiny strings of love bond us like cobwebs,
See it in my eyes: - true intimate love,
That can drive you to your wildest fantasies,
My glees are of truth with the reason being: -
That our differences are sold and cast out,
I love you with passion, like any sweet-scented flower,
For I want your heart to beat with mine,
And the warm breath from your nose find my chest to moist.

SHIPWRECK

In my many dreams, it's your grotesque I could see,
The woo and the charm that would provoke me to flee,
But in my weakness and the strength of your glaring eyes,
Sabotaging me and conforming me to fit in your angular cocoon,
Confusing my sight, all I could see are reds and maroons,
I am lost, and desolate. I can't tell of anything I used to know,
I can't breathe when you place your phalanges on my chest,
Creating commotions with my nerves: - again I can't breathe,

You drag me by my skin to the deepest part of your dungeon,

To the darkest place I've never been,

where your demons reside,

In my fright and my tight closed eyes,
I could hear sounds, echoes,
Am lost, gone, thwarted in the murky mud of merrymaking.

fifty-nine years ago, time like this, someone was born,
unselfish person of good character,
someone who's kindness is formidable and rare,
i know good heavens, were stalled in sanguine awe,
even my dad, that day had a good dream,
someone so wealthy of physical and emotional energy,
through you i've learnt ways of He who is almighty,
you taught me to fight my personal strife,
and face earthly tough luck,
i stood by and waited, this day,
to scribble a piece for you, i'd write a whole novel,
but am frail, so week to try, smile mommy,
this time broader with elation,
for this is a great day for you: your birthday

SOFT HEART OF A POET

If you break a poet's heart you break the world into tears,
If you make a poet crawl in pain you make as all fierce,
If you make a poet's hopes crush, their dreams you disperse,
Scattering them into a void so hollow, redemption is scarce,

If you break a poet's heart, your conscience derails,
If you break a poet's heart you take their decree to veil,
If you make a poet's hopes crush you make dreams frail,
Scattering them into a world so deep, resurrection surreal,

If you break a poet's heart you will cry some time in pain,
Standing in the dark watching your tears washed in the rain,
Then imagine your frail soul now entangled with a chain,
And regret why you break a poet's heart in vain,
Time you glare at yourself with a cross between fury and disdain.

In my deep annotations, I had no rights to woo you,
But… but I stretched myself and took you anyway,
Now I love what has become of you, the you I see,
In the gleam of every dark night, fate is a fickle, a whore,
I like it in me that I love you, let her judge my misgivings, And my
worriment, for I can't relent of your meekness,
Softer than sounds and smells.

I tremble in my writing, not because am old,
I took this time, not 'cause I had enough for waste,
scribbling again, not 'cause i've not written enough for you,
as I sort a brief caricature of you in my busy brain,
Dripping my ink in this piece of white just for her,
Telling of her beauty that folds this spell of love in my heart,
my guardian of passionate love , queen of caress and sweet words.

The boy i thought i barely knew,
has brought me a feeling i term as new,
so sober and fresh more than even you,
let him say if I've bitten more than i can chew,
i bet it's not a game of lose and chances,
I beseech you, choose wisely ignore the masses,
my heart is bare as bald touch and feel the paces,
now you know indeed am keen on trespasses,
it's your heart i crawl for, nothing else to fight for,

I saw a princess in my good dreams,
Glaring intimately with much splendor
I wanted to woo because am a charmer,
She stared with innocence, her smile can shame the stars,
I envy the curves formed from her smiles,
Daughter of the kings I've traveled many miles,
To touch those silk hair and drink from your dewy cup,
To appreciate the taste of your sweet nectary sap,
Before I trudge with you on my journey so long,
To the sons and daughters of the soil, I long,

Minutes before I see the snowy light flowers,
And the tiny watery drops from the corners of my eyes,
Setting sail my dhow to a journey so long,
Stiff, numb, mumbling and motionless,
Then I'll know it's time to walk behind the skies,
Flashing before my sight, earthly good and bad doings,

Ready to leap over the thorny pied in my 80's or 90's,
And now the screams, the bull's billows renting air space,
Drop no tear, let *lesse* hold this and shout it to all who came,
Tell them how much my world to you was fame,
Before lowering to the four corner six deep,
I know I'll force a smile in my slumber because I made peace,
Dusted the prints with those who owed me and I owed.

STOLEN INNOCENCE

That evening, I watched the wind swayed trees,
And the clouds bowing to the setting sun,
I lost a good friend, that I've had since birth,
His smile strangled all the butterflies in my stomach,
I saw it all in his eyes, the thirst, the last and the urge,
I was weak, defenseless and lost, he charmed me,
I loved him from one to infinity,
He glided like a python with its tongue stitched out,
Appreciated my well mounded honey pot,
He drunk it, all of it, the honey in my pot,
I felt something warm all over my face
He deceived me! He stole from me, he spilled my honey away,
Now am here hollow, dark, like the inside of an abyss,
The sweet sweeping sounds of the palms are my only console.

I'M CAPTIVATED

Your love has entangled me in bush wrap chains
An antidote that melts all my worries and pains
Your love is like a melody when I hum, it pays
Two is prettier than solo for the almighty says
Slide your fingers in mine, lets watch the stars together
Warm my heart with your sweet voice am sure it won't wither
I drip my ink for I love you, cross my heart I won't dither,
When I met you, I knew we'd care for each other,
If your love surpasses my own then I'll feel it in my shivers,
I'll get crazy 'bout you, the world should just leave us,
You evoked my untouched parts, baby you're so callous,
Your smile that breezes my pores is so precious,
Whenever you smile am detained, I lose my speak,
Am meek and I reap from the gardens of your wonderfulness

good heart, clean soul, adorning smile,
that's what i see in your eyes when you stare,
the soft, meek and feathery look touched my heart,
very deep to the fibres, and the thin tendons,
i tried to evade with might but your became my weakness,
draining me with weariness, warming my heart like a prayer in paradise,
let me experience more of your leafy touch and deep look,
spark my heart with kind words and more laughter,
and a beautiful smile in a sea of grim faces,
let me watch you in your sweet slumber and share your fantasies,
watch your wake in the cold of dawn and the beam of morning sun,
let me hold you and then read my lips.... I LOVE YOU

MY INEFFICACY

During the deep dark days when you left,
My beating heart disturbed like victim of theft,
Savaged like beasts in the southern mountains,
The dazzling diva had an elaborate plan in place,
The space in my heart hollow and emptied by the world,
Lost in the desolation of space and time,
The word disappointment haunting my thoughts,
Clenching my teeth, rage seeping from my pores,
Your words that made butterflies collide in my stomach,
Vanished seamlessly, my queen of caress and sweet words,
My heart sunk to the pit of my stomach,
Chills that raised hair on my sheen,
And the butterflies subsided in disbelief,
On the verge of tears, healing is history,
It felt like stabbing of spite, when I couldn't yield to your might.

I want to let you know, surpassing all odds,
That this day is one of those I can't afford to forget,
One of which I didn't know somehow we would connect,
But all the same your love I promised I will protect,
Your agility and bliss filled my heart with contentment,

I want to let you know, surpassing all odds,
That our inequities rhymed and fitted like a jigsaw,
I knew we matched, love pure and white like a snow,
Your deep love swayed me and made me drool somehow,
This day that we celebrate our anniversary with a bow,

I want to let you know, surpassing all odds,
from word to word I can tell of our merry moments, if there's need,
Even the stars that seeks mercy of light from the sun,
Is witnessing this moment with a heartfelt mead,
stand by you and shun those who despise you with a pan,

The rising sun, the chipping birds, the dewy grass,
You, your bliss, your charm, your unseen beings,
You surge, i'm weak, drained like an old medieval sculpture,
Your words thwart me into a delicious Frenzy,
And then your unseen beings, pruning me hair by hair,
Sliding along the silkiness of your spicy nothings,
Your embrace, cutting through my flaws and imperfections,
Each turn of your chapter drapes me deeper,
You, your bliss, your charm, your unseen beings,
Entangles me into a befitting chamber,
I can't recollect, I can't fathom, this is the new home.

A DARK NIGHT, A HOLLOW PLACE

Last night, in my bed, while asleep,
I had a dream, about myself drenched,
Soaked, wet in something I don't know of,
I had a gory dream, of myself inside of an abyss,
I was falling fast, the darkness of it,
Embracing me with last, wagging its tongue like a serpent,
Roaring in hunger, wanting more of me, all of me,
That was sad, I got scared, what have I gotten Into?
This is deep, very deep, it's a bottomless pit,
It's an abyss, dark like under the bed.

The lust, the lurk, the lure, the envy,
all that is merry, yummy and tasty,
The pure, the sinning, the holier, the bliss,
All that are glamorous, their eyes, their fuss,
The bold, the beautiful, their drench, the muddle,
All those weak, their fear, my advantage,
The lies, the love, their weak spot, my loophole,
All that I garner, from the chat walls, my trophies,
Their silhouettes, their dirt, their spirits, my soul,
The restlessness, the urge, the compulsions, the voices,
Now the wake, after the stupor, my cleansing in the offing,
Finally, my redemption, the ecdysis, the relief and all...

That evening we fought our resistance,
between thoughts of dos and donts,
and then touch of skin smooth and lean,
that probed me to stack my tongue out,
barrowing through to your navel,
as we piece by piece removed our clothes,
and they found a resting place on the floor,
until there were no hiding places,
for the two yearning and wanting bodies,

passion revealed in this hot moment,
i glided further to your honey pot,
a gasp broke the soothing moan,
until there was no room to hold it anymore,
as i moved atop of you with ease,
and then skin twined with skin,
a demanding thrust of passion revealed,
as we forced our way to the peak of ecstasy.

THE END